Text STYLES

HOW TO WRITE A DRAMA

Megan Kopp

Crabtree Publishing Company
www.crabtreebooks.com

Text STYLES

Author: Megan Kopp

Publishing plan research and series development: Reagan Miller

Editor: Anastasia Suen

Proofreader: Wendy Scavuzzo

Logo design: Samantha Crabtree

Print coordinator: Katherine Berti

Production coordinator and prepress technician: Margaret Amy Salter

Photographs:

Shutterstock: Sergey Kamshylin: pages 20 (bottom), 21 (bottom left and center); Maljalen: page 21 (bottom right)

All other images by Shutterstock

Library and Archives Canada Cataloguing in Publication

Kopp, Megan, author
How to write a drama / Megan Kopp.

(Text styles)
Includes index.
Issued in print and electronic formats.
ISBN 978-0-7787-1653-2 (bound).--
ISBN 978-0-7787-1658-7 (pbk.).--
ISBN 978-1-4271-9863-1 (pdf).--
ISBN 978-1-4271-9868-6 (html)

1. Playwriting--Juvenile literature. I. Title. II. Series: Text styles

PN1661.K56 2014 j808.2 C2014-903770-8
C2014-903771-6

Library of Congress Cataloging-in-Publication Data

Kopp, Megan, author.
How to write a drama / Megan Kopp.
pages cm. -- (Text styles)
Includes index.
ISBN 978-0-7787-1653-2 (reinforced library binding) --
ISBN 978-0-7787-1658-7 (pbk.) --
ISBN 978-1-4271-9863-1 (electronic pdf) --
ISBN 978-1-4271-9868-6 (electronic html)
1. Playwriting--Juvenile literature. I. Title.

PN1661.K57 2014
808.2--dc23

2014022774

Crabtree Publishing Company

Printed in Canada/022023/CPC20230216

www.crabtreebooks.com 1-800-387-7650

 In Canada: We acknowledge the financial support of the Government of Canada through the Canada Book Fund for our publishing activities.

Published in Canada
Crabtree Publishing
616 Welland Ave.
St. Catharines, Ontario
L2M 5V6

Published in the United States
Crabtree Publishing
347 Fifth Ave
Suite 1402-145
New York, NY 10016

Published in the United Kingdom
Crabtree Publishing
Maritime House
Basin Road North, Hove
BN41 1WR

Published in Australia
Crabtree Publishing
Unit 3-5
Currumbin Court
Capalaba QLD 4157

Contents

What Is Drama?

"To be, or not to be…" That is **drama**, or rather Shakespeare's drama! Drama is simply a piece of writing that tells a story. It is often serious and not usually meant to make readers laugh. Dramas usually tell a story about events in the life of a **character**.

The word "drama" comes from a Greek word meaning "to do." Drama is often linked with the idea of action. It is written for performance on stage, in a movie, on television, or voiced on radio. Drama is writing that is meant to be seen or heard, not just read.

Have you ever acted out a story with your friends? Have you ever watched a play on a stage? These are examples of drama. Drama is found in countries all over the world.

Common elements of a drama are:

- Drama is a story that is acted out in front of an audience.
- There are often three acts in a drama.
- In the first act the characters and a problem are introduced.
- In the middle act, interest and tension are built.
- In the final act, everything is wrapped up.
- Drama is written in a special format called a script.
- The script builds a picture of what is happening on stage.
- The script includes a list of characters, lines the characters say, and stage directions.

Drama has deep roots! The first record of drama was from a religious festival in Ancient Greece. This was around 600 B.C.E. Aristotle was a famous Greek thinker. He wrote a book called *Poetics* on how to make a good drama.

William Shakespeare was born in 1564. He was an actor and a poet who wrote plays. His dramas are studied and performed all over the world, even today. Ever heard of "Romeo and Juliet"?

Writing One Scene As Poetry, Prose, and Drama

Dramas often include a flaw in the main character. A common flaw is too much pride. In Greek dramas, the main character starts out with a good life. Something happens because of the character's flaw. The character must realize what is happening and grow or change.

Drama tells a story or describes an event much like **prose**. Prose relies heavily on description. Drama relies on **dialogue** to tell the story. In prose, the characters' relationships are revealed slowly through the story. **Poetry** differs from both drama and prose. It uses the sound of words to create a musical effect.

Poem

Kate would not get out of her bed

Her mother tried to raise her head

"It's time, it's time," Mother did say

But Kate thought it was best to stay

Prose

Kate's mother was frantic. It was time for Kate to get up for school and she was still in bed.

"Kate, you must get up," Mother said again.

"I will, I will, just give me a minute," said Kate.

Drama

MOTHER: Kate, Kate, get up!

KATE: By and by, mother.

MOTHER: It is time to go to school. Get up!

KATE: By and by, mother, by and by.

In this book, you will learn about all of the characteristics of drama. You will read some short dramas and even write a drama of your own!

Lazy Kate

~ a drama by Augusta Stevenson

SCENE 1

TIME: *early in the morning.*
PLACE: *Kate's bedroom.*
CHARACTERS: KATE
MOTHER
BED

[KATE *is in bed. Her* MOTHER *comes in.*]
MOTHER: Kate, Kate, get up!
KATE: By and by, mother.
MOTHER: It is time to go to school. Get up!
KATE: By and by, mother, by and by.
MOTHER: You will be late to school, I fear.
[*The* MOTHER *goes out.*]
BED: Dear me! Dear me! Kate will not get up. Well, she shall not be late to school. I will see to that.
[*The* BED *walks from the room into the street.* KATE *is frightened.*]
KATE: Bed, Bed, where are you going?
BED: To school, you lazy child.

SCENE 2

TIME: *five minutes later.*
PLACE: *the schoolroom.*
CHARACTERS: KATE
TEACHER
BED
BOYS AND GIRLS

[*The* BED *enters the schoolroom.* KATE *tries to hide under the covers.*]
BED: Good-morning, teacher. Here is lazy Kate.
TEACHER: Ha, ha, ha!
BED: Good-morning, boys. Here is lazy Kate.

BOYS: Ha, ha, ha!
BED: Good-morning, girls. Here is lazy Kate.
GIRLS: Ha, ha, ha!
KATE: Take me home, Bed! Please take me home!
BED: Will you get up early?
KATE: O yes, yes, yes!
BED: Every morning?
KATE: Every morning, Bed! Every morning!
BED: Then I will take you home. Good-by, teacher!
TEACHER: Ha, ha, ha!
BED: Good-by, children!
CHILDREN: Ha, ha, ha!
[*The* BED *goes with* KATE, *who still tries to hide under the covers.*]

SCENE 3

TIME: *two minutes later.*
PLACE: *Kate's bedroom.*
CHARACTERS: KATE
MOTHER

[KATE *is asleep. Her* MOTHER *comes in.*]
MOTHER: Kate, Kate! You are asleep again! Get up and go to school!
KATE: I have been to school.
MOTHER: What is this?
KATE: I have been to school. The Bed took me.
MOTHER: You have been dreaming, child.
KATE: No, no! The Bed took me to school. The children laughed at me.
MOTHER: It was a dream, my dear.
KATE: Well, I promised the Bed to get up early. I know that was not a dream.
[*She jumps out of bed.*]
MOTHER: Oh, that is fine!
KATE: I must not be late to school. I promised the Bed.

Dramatic Characters

A character is anyone who appears in a story.

A trait is part of a character's personality.

Dramas list characters at the beginning of the play. The characters in *Lazy Kate* include Kate, Bed, Mother, Teacher, Boys, and Girls. Kate is the main character. The main characters in dramas often have an important trait, or characteristic.

In dramas, this trait is often a flaw. The flaw helps drive the story. Kate's flaw is that she is lazy. We discover this trait by looking at the script. Read the sentences below.

MOTHER: Kate, Kate, get up!

KATE: By and by, mother.

MOTHER: It is time to go to school. Get up!

KATE: By and by, mother, by and by.

Kate is in bed. She's going to be late for school. Her mother asks her twice to get up. Twice Kate replies that she will, eventually!

We do not know much about Bed. It's just a bed – that talks and walks! Bed also has character traits. Bed is determined. Bed won't quit until it teaches Kate a lesson. The phrase "Here is lazy Kate" is repeated three times when Bed takes Kate to school. Bed is not afraid to embarrass Kate in front of her classmates to make a point.

?

Characters often grow or change in a drama. Conflict **is a big part of drama. Characters face conflict and must overcome it. How does Kate grow or change in this drama?**

Brainstorming Characters

Think of a few characters for your own drama. What are their names? How old are they in this story? What are their relationships with other characters in the story? What traits or character flaws do they have? Are they ambitious? Are they unable to focus on one task? Are they greedy? Write down a list of characters and notes about them. Do not worry about thinking of a lot of characters. Focus on creating a few good-quality characters. You can use familiar characters.

Dialogue: Spoken Better Than Shakespeare

When a character speaks in a drama, it is called dialogue. Dialogue brings the story to life. Dialogue is conversation.

This conversation can be between two or more characters. It can be between one character and an audience. When one character does all of the talking, it is called a **monologue**.

KATE: Bed, Bed, where are you going?

BED: To school, you lazy child.

This is a problem for Kate. How is her problem solved? By dialogue, of course!

KATE: Take me home, Bed! Please take me home!

BED: Will you get up early?

KATE: O yes, yes, yes!

BED: Every morning?

KATE: Every morning, Bed! Every morning!

BED: Then I will take you home.

In a book, dialogue is shown by putting quotation marks (" ") around the words that are spoken. In a drama, the character's name comes at the front of the sentence they will speak.

Books differ from dramas because the conversation is often separated by pieces of description. These bits of writing show the reader what is happening. That isn't necessary in a drama, because the audience is seeing what is going on. They don't need to read it.

Dialogue can show what the character is thinking or feeling. It helps move the story along. Dialogue can set up conflict and provide a solution.

Now It's Your Turn

Add some more dialogue to the drama *Lazy Kate* on the next morning when Kate's mother comes to wake her up. What does Kate have to say? Does Bed have any more words left to speak?

Stage Directions: Where, Oh Where?

The **setting** is important in writing stories. In drama, the characters are usually more important than the setting. Their movements on stage help express emotion. Physical movement helps move the story forward. In drama, these movements are written as stage directions.

Stage directions tell the characters what to do. They can tell the characters where to go on stage, how to move, and how they should say their lines.

[*The* BED *walks from the room into the street.* KATE *is frightened.*]

[KATE *is in bed. Her* MOTHER *comes in.*]

Notice how these stage directions include setting details. The setting is where your story takes place. In *Lazy Kate*, the first setting is her bedroom. These stage directions show that Bed walks out of the bedroom and into the street. They also show how the characters should react to what is happening. How do you think the actor playing Kate would use actions to show that they are frightened?

Write down the setting for your own drama. Describe it. Is it set outside in a park or indoors in a school gymnasium? If outdoors, is the sun shining or is it cloudy? What does the park look like? Is it a wild space or is the grass mowed for outdoor recreation? Little details are very important. They help the writing become clear and interesting for the reader. Settings may change with each new act. Write down the setting place and time for every new act. When something changes in a scene, record it.

Dramatic Plots: Say What?

The plot is what happens in a story. Plots always start with a problem. This is the beginning. The main character has a problem and must find a way to solve it. The problem is also called conflict. Conflict comes in the middle of the drama. The climax is the moment of most excitement. Somehow, the problem gets solved. This is the resolution.

A Problem for a Drama

Choose a character for a drama. What does the character want? How does the character get it? Explain how your character will solve that problem. Be creative. Save this idea to use in your own drama.

In *Lazy Kate*, the first act introduces Kate, her mother and Bed. It sets up the fact that Kate does not want to get up and go to school. It also shows that Bed is going to make her go. This is the conflict.

In the middle, interest is built up as Bed takes her into the classroom. Tension builds as the teacher and students start to laugh.

In the final act, Kate jumps out of bed as soon as her mother comes into the room. She has learned her lesson.

Think Beginning, Middle, End

Reread one of your favorite books. Pretend you are going to write this book as a short drama. Use a couple of sentences to answer each of the following questions:

What happens in the beginning?

How is interest and tension built up?

What happens to close the story (or drama!)?

Story Map for *Lazy Kate*

Characters

- Kate, Bed, Kate's mother, teacher, boys and girls

Settings

- bedroom and schoolroom

Problem

- Kate is lazy and does not want to get out of bed

Events

1. Kate's mother comes into room but Kate does not want to get up yet.
2. Mother leaves.
3. Bed walks out of bedroom with Kate and into classroom.
4. Teacher and students laugh and Kate is embarrassed.
5. Kate tells Bed she wants to go home and promises to get up every morning.
6. Bed takes Kate home.
7. Mother enters room and wakes up Kate telling her she was dreaming.
8. Climax: Kate jumps out of bed and says she must not be late for school.

Resolution

- Kate gets up every morning and is not late for school.

Lesson

- Kate learns not to be lazy because it will be embarrassing.

Theme: What Is the Matter?

The theme **is the lesson or message of the drama. Characters in dramas must overcome a problem of some kind. These problems can be an internal battle, or they can relate to others around them. Dramas show this conflict through words and actions.**

Drama helps readers and observers learn more about themselves. In an indirect way, it can show people how they might act in a particular situation.

- **Sometimes the theme is very clear. In *Lazy Kate*, the theme is suggested in the title. Theme: Don't be lazy because it will embarrass you.**
- **In other dramas, you will need to watch carefully to uncover the theme. What do the characters say and do? What happens as a result of their actions? How do the characters change?**

Theme Detective

You have a mystery to solve. Look at the fairytale of *Goldilocks and the Three Bears*. **What is the theme of this story? Write down your answers.**

Creative Response to the Drama

The Daily News

EXTRA! EXTRA!

Read All About It!

Write a short newspaper article describing the drama's plot and characters. Summarize what happens in the drama and tell readers a little bit about the characters.

Put It in a Letter

Choose a character and write a letter from their perspective. Perhaps the character is writing to one of their parents, or to a loved one, or a best friend, trying to explain something they've done.

It can be something directly relating to the story, an event that happened in the past, or maybe it's a secret that the character is revealing for the first time.

Picture This Character!

Look through magazines to find a picture of one of your drama's characters. Mount the photograph of the person along with photos of some of the person's favorite things, expressions, and places. Make sure you give your character a name.

The Emperor's Test

~ a condensed version of a drama by Augusta Stevenson

SCENE I

TIME: *one spring; noon.*

PLACE: *an army camp on the banks of a large creek. A village is nearby. To the south is a great forest.*

THE EMPEROR; THE GENERAL; THE CAPTAIN; THE MAYOR'S WIFE AND SON; THE RICH MERCHANT'S WIFE AND SON; THE POOR WOODCUTTER'S WIFE AND HER SON, PIERRE

[*Enter the* MAYOR'S WIFE *and* SON; *the* RICH MERCHANT'S WIFE *and* SON.]

GENERAL: You have come to see the Emperor?

THE LADIES: General, we have.

GENERAL: His Majesty wishes you to leave your sons here in camp until evening.

MAYOR'S WIFE: General, could you not tell us the Emperor's plans?

GENERAL: Yes, madam. The Emperor must march southward where the enemy is in camp. He wishes a guide who can lead him safely through this great forest.

RICH MERCHANT'S WIFE: We were told the Emperor would greatly honor the lad he chooses.

GENERAL: It is true, madam. The lad chosen will be made an aide.

MAYOR'S WIFE: But how will the Emperor make a choice?

GENERAL: A test will be given every boy who comes. This test will prove his fitness to be guide.

[*The* GENERAL *bows to the ladies and leaves.*]

[*Enter the* POOR WOODCUTTER'S WIFE *and* SON.]

POOR WOODCUTTER'S WIFE (*timidly*): I heard the Emperor wanted a guide.

MAYOR'S WIFE: The Emperor only wants the boys of the best families, madam.

[*Enter the* EMPEROR, GENERAL, *and* CAPTAIN; *they remain back; are not seen by the ladies.*]

POOR WOODCUTTER'S WIFE (*sighing*): I suppose that is true, but Pierre is a smart boy. If the Emperor could only see him—

RICH MERCHANT'S WIFE (*interrupting*): The Emperor wants a boy with proud manners such as our boys have.

EMPEROR (*indignantly*): Fiddlesticks!

THE LADIES (*bowing*): Your Highness!

EMPEROR: Fiddlesticks and candles, I say!

POOR WOODCUTTER'S WIFE: I am sorry, your Majesty. I didn't know how it was. Come, Pierre.

[*She turns to go.*]

EMPEROR: Remain. Pierre shall have the test with the others. Ladies, you shall know whom I have chosen when the test is finished. I bid you good-day.

[*The ladies bow and go.*]

EMPEROR (*turning to the boys*): My lads, go through the forest southward, till you come to the river. You may then return. Captain, see that guards go with them. My lads, you must not speak the one to the other until I have again seen you. I must have your word on that. Do you promise?

BOYS: Sire, we promise.

EMPEROR: Captain, they are now in your charge. General, a word with you.
[*The* EMPEROR *and* GENERAL *exit. The* CAPTAIN *leads the boys away.*]

SCENE II

TIME: *two hours later.*
PLACE: *the Emperor's tent; the Emperor's room.*
THE EMPEROR, FIRST AIDE, SECOND AIDE, LUDWIG

[*The* EMPEROR *is seen sitting at a table looking at maps. Enter an* AIDE. *He salutes.*]
EMPEROR: Well?
AIDE: The prisoner has returned, sire.
EMPEROR: What prisoner?
AIDE: The one sent out for the test, sire.
EMPEROR: Ah, yes; bid him enter.
[AIDE *goes; he reenters with* LUDWIG, *who wears an old, torn army cloak over his uniform. He salutes.*]
I notice you are a bit lame, Ludwig.
LUDWIG: Yes, sire; in my left leg. My dog was hit at the same time.
EMPEROR: Does your dog go to battle with you?
LUDWIG: If he can slip into the ranks, sire. He always goes where I go, sire.
EMPEROR: Then he went with you today, of course?
LUDWIG: Yes, sire.
EMPEROR: You are sure the boys didn't see you?
LUDWIG: No one saw me. I kept a sharp lookout. When I came to a clear space I went to one side, hiding behind trees, to look ahead. Then I ran across.
EMPEROR: That must have tired you, Ludwig. You're not quite well yet.
LUDWIG: I found I couldn't leap the streams; I had to climb down the banks and wade them.
EMPEROR: You rested by the way, didn't you?
LUDWIG: Yes, sire, and once I stopped to pick berries.
EMPEROR: You made the return trip by boat up the creek?
LUDWIG: Yes, sire.
EMPEROR: That is all.
[*The* AIDE *and* LUDWIG *go.*]

SCENE III

TIME: *a half hour later.*
PLACE: *the Emperor's tent; the ante-room.*
THE EMPEROR; THE GENERAL; THE CAPTAIN; AN AIDE; THE MAYOR'S WIFE AND SON; THE RICH MERCHANT'S WIFE AND SON; THE POOR WOODCUTTER'S WIFE AND SON, PIERRE

[*The ladies wait in the lower end of ante-room. Back is a great armchair.*]
MAYOR'S WIFE: I cannot think why the boys were sent into the forest!
RICH MERCHANT'S WIFE: Nor I! It seems to me the Emperor should have asked them what they could do. Now, my boy dances so prettily!
MAYOR'S WIFE: I was certain he would ask them to ride. Now, my boy rides so well—just like a prince!

RICH MERCHANT'S WIFE: Well, he will no doubt ask them all these things upon their return.

[*She turns to Pierre's mother.*]

You see, madam, how little chance your boy has. I am sure he cannot dance?

POOR WOODCUTTER'S WIFE (*sadly*): No, madam.

MAYOR'S WIFE: I am certain he does not ride?

POOR WOODCUTTER'S WIFE (*sighing*): No, madam.

[*Enter an* AIDE; *crosses to Emperor's room; announces at curtains.*]

AIDE: The boys have returned, sire!

[*Enter the* CAPTAIN *with the* BOYS. *Enter the* GENERAL *from Emperor's room.*]

GENERAL (*announcing*): The Emperor!

[*Enter the* EMPEROR; *all bow.*]

EMPEROR (*sitting in armchair*): I will now give the test. Captain, bring up the first boy.

[*The* CAPTAIN *brings up the* RICH MERCHANT'S SON.]

EMPEROR: Well, my lad, what did you see in the forest?

RICH MERCHANT'S SON: Many, many trees, sire.

EMPEROR: You saw nothing but trees?

RICH MERCHANT'S SON: That was all, sire—just trees.

EMPEROR: I shall not want you; you may go.

RICH MERCHANT'S WIFE: Oh, your Majesty, if you could only see him dance!

EMPEROR: Candles and cheese! Do I want a dancing guide? Captain, bring up the next one.

[*The* CAPTAIN *brings up the* MAYOR'S SON.]

EMPEROR: Well, my lad, what did you see in the forest?

MAYOR'S SON: I saw trees and bushes, sire.

EMPEROR: Nothing more?

MAYOR'S SON: No, sire.

EMPEROR: I shall not want you; you may go.

MAYOR'S WIFE: Oh, your Majesty, if you could only see him ride! Just like a prince, sire!

EMPEROR: Fiddlesticks! Captain, the last boy there.

[*The* CAPTAIN *brings up* PIERRE].

EMPEROR: Well, my lad, what did you see in the forest?

PIERRE: I saw that a man had passed southward just before us, sire.

EMPEROR: How did you know that? Did you see him?

PIERRE: No, sire, I saw his footprints. He was lame in the left leg.

EMPEROR: How did you learn that?

PIERRE. The footprints were deeper on the right side. His dog was lame also.

EMPEROR: He had a dog?

PIERRE: Yes, sire; a lame dog I'm sure, because one of his tracks was always faint or missing.

EMPEROR: Did you trace this man and dog by their footprints?

PIERRE: Yes, sire, to the river. I am certain they had passed but a short time before—not more than a half hour.

EMPEROR. How could you tell that?

PIERRE: The grass had not yet straightened up. The tracks in the mud had not yet filled with water. The prints in the dust were still clear although a wind was blowing. The rocks were still damp.

EMPEROR: Good! Very good!

PIERRE: Sire, I fear this man is one of the enemy!

EMPEROR: Indeed! What proof have you of that?

PIERRE: This, sire.

[*Handing a small piece of cloth to* EMPEROR.]

It is the color of the enemy's uniform.

EMPEROR: It is, my lad. How came you by it?

PIERRE: I found it on a thorn-bush. It was torn from his cloak, sire.

EMPEROR: And why from his cloak?

PIERRE: The thorn-bush was at least three feet from the man's line of travel. The wind blew the cloak about.

EMPEROR: Well, Pierre, do you think we should be in fear of this enemy?

PIERRE: I do not know, sire. I only know that he has a good disposition.

EMPEROR (*surprised*): A good disposition? How do you know that?

PIERRE: The dog was always near him. When the man stopped to rest, the dog lay down at his feet.

EMPEROR: But he may have held the dog there, my lad.

PIERRE: Not while he was picking berries, sire.

EMPEROR: So our enemy picked berries, did he?

PIERRE: Yes, sire, the dog lying by the bushes all the while.

EMPEROR: Do you think we could capture this man?

PIERRE: Yes, sire, for he was very tired.

EMPEROR: How do you know that?

PIERRE: He climbed down the banks of every small stream. I should have leaped them.

EMPEROR: You think it would be an easy matter, then, to follow and capture him?

PIERRE: Not easy, sire, for he was always on the lookout.

EMPEROR: How do you know that?

PIERRE: Whenever he reached a clear space, he went to one side, hiding behind trees to look ahead. Then he ran across the open.

EMPEROR: Your proof of this, my lad?

PIERRE: His footprints in every clear space showed only the balls of the feet.

EMPEROR: Good! You followed him only to the river.

PIERRE: Those were the orders, sire. Had I gone on, I could have overtaken him by evening.

EMPEROR: That you could not, my lad, for the man is now here, in camp. He returned by boat. Ladies, the test is over.

[*He turns to Pierre's mother.*]

Madam, your son shall be my guide. I am proud to have a boy of such keen sight and quick thought in my kingdom. And 't is much to be the mother of such a lad. I salute you, madam!

[*He bows to the happy woman with great courtesy.*]

The Drama Is in the Characters

The Emperor's Test has many characters. Most play a supporting role to the Emperor and Pierre. These are the two main characters. The Emperor needs to find a good guide. Pierre needs to prove himself worthy of the position, even though he is from a poor family.

The drama comes as we watch the boys fail, one by one. What hope does Pierre have? Interest is captured the moment he starts showing his tracking talents. Pierre works hard to pass the Emperor's test.

What character traits does Pierre show? What character traits do the other boys have? Do you feel Pierre should have won the Emperor's test?

Compare and Contrast

When you compare two things, you are looking at how they are alike. When you contrast them, you are looking at how they are different. Fill in the table below to show how these two minor characters are alike and how they are different.

	Differences	Similarities
Mayor's Wife		
Poor Woodcutter's Wife		

Dialogue: Talk the Talk

Dialogue is a special kind of action in which someone is talking. A play is a story with almost nothing but talking. As the characters talk, the story moves along. Dialogue is a useful tool for building settings and developing characters.

In *The Emperor's Test*, the mothers bring out the conflict in their opening discussion about what the Emperor needs in an aide. Pierre's mother is scorned by the other mothers. Her son cannot dance or ride a horse. A minor conflict arises about son will win the test.

Draw a Venn diagram to compare and contrast the dialogue in *The Emperor's Test* with the dialogue in *Lazy Kate*. Write ten words that are used in both dramas. Write ten words that are different in each drama. Do any of these different words give you a better understanding of the characters and what is important to them? Write a few paragraphs to share your discoveries.

Consider the potential characters for your own drama. How would they talk? Write a short conversation between your two main characters as they talk about their favorite movies and why they enjoyed them.

Stage Directions: Set in Place

An entire drama can revolve around a character's struggle. Settings for dramas can be as simple as a chair, a park bench, or a car. Stage directions can show a character who is upset by having them stand up, sit down, and move around the chair.

Stage directions are normally placed in parentheses ( ) for an individual character's stage directions. Brackets [ ] are used for stage directions that have more than one character.

GENERAL (*announcing*): The Emperor!

[*Enter the* EMPEROR; *all bow.*]

Stage directions can show the emotion used to speak the words.

POOR WOODCUTTER'S WIFE (*timidly*): I heard the Emperor wanted a guide.

EMPEROR (*surprised*): A good disposition? How do you know that?

The stage directions for *The Emperor's Test* are simple.

The AIDE *and* LUDWIG *go. The* CAPTAIN *brings up* PIERRE.

These simple stage directions don't show conflict. They help by providing a setting. They also keep the play moving forward.

Change It Up!

Write a description of stage directions ***for The Emperor's Test*** **as though the entire drama were set in a school.**

Dramatic Plots: Mapping the Story

Discuss the plot of *The Emperor's Test.*

What happens in the middle part of this story? What lesson is learned in the end?

Story Map for *The Emperor's Test*

Characters

- Emperor, General, Captain, Aides, Ludwig, Rich Merchant's Wife, Rich Merchant's Son, Mayor's Wife, Mayor's Son, Poor Woodcutter's Wife, Pierre

Settings

- Emperor's tent, Emperor's room, ante-room

Problem

- Pierre must prove he is smart enough to become the Emperor's guide.

Events

1. Mothers bring their sons for the Emperor's test for a new guide.
2. The Emperor sends a prisoner through the woods to set a trail.
3. The boys are sent out into the woods to see what they can see.
4. The boys return and the Emperor asks what they have spotted.
5. Two boys see nothing but trees and bushes.
6. Pierre describes the route of the prisoner perfectly.
7. The Emperor is impressed and gives Pierre the job.

Resolution

- Pierre gets the job over the wealthy boys.

Lesson

- Hard work is rewarded.

Theme: What Is It About?

Drama brings us closer to "real" life problems because it allows us to observe "make-believe" conflict from a safe distance. All dramas have a message of some sort. That message is the theme. The theme might be a **moral,** if the drama is written to include one. Themes can usually be summarized in one sentence.

The theme of *The Emperor's Test* is: "Hard work is rewarded." Pierre is a poor woodcutter's son. He does not have the same privileges as the sons of wealthy families. Pierre doesn't expect anything. He simply does the task he is asked to do. He does it to the very best of his ability. As a result, he astounds the Emperor with his knowledge of tracking. He is rewarded with the prized position as the Emperor's guide.

In the drama *Lazy Kate*, the theme is: "Don't be lazy or it will embarrass you." On one hand, these two themes seem quite different from each other. One focuses on hard work. The other highlights laziness. These two themes are actually quite similar in nature. Both suggest that laziness is not a good thing. Getting the job done is good. You feel better and this is a reward.

In small groups, discuss the themes of *The Emperor's Test* and *Lazy Kate*. How are they similar? How do they differ? Could you use either of the two themes for your own drama? Why or why not?

Creative Response to the Drama

Draw a Character with Words!

Draw an outline of a person on a large sheet of paper. Describe your character with words (e.g., big feet, long hair, brown hair, brown eyes…) and write these words on and around the outline. You can include physical appearance, age, male or female, in school or working (describe job). You can also include the character's likes and dislikes, friends and enemies, and secrets and dreams.

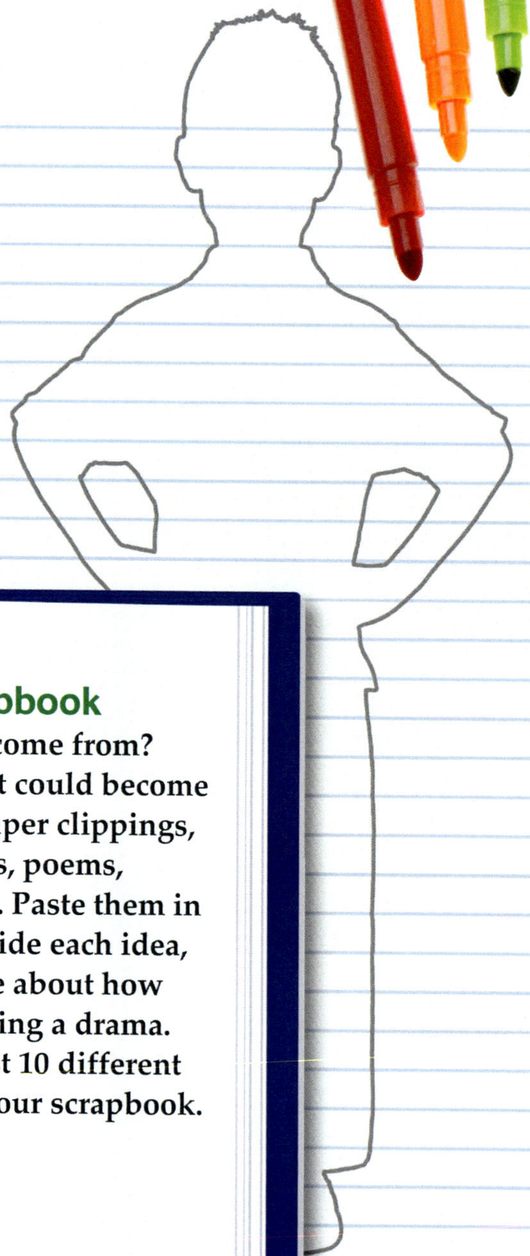

Plot Starters

Can't think of what to write? Start writing a plot for your drama with:

It would be interesting if…

Why does…

I remember…

Create a Scrapbook

Where do ideas come from? Collect ideas that could become a drama (newspaper clippings, magazine articles, poems, songs, photos…). Paste them in a scrapbook. Beside each idea, write a brief note about how you see it becoming a drama. Try to add at least 10 different things/ideas to your scrapbook.

Writing a Drama

You've learned all about characters, dialogue, stage directions, and plots. Now write your own drama.

1

Before the Drama Begins

Dramas rely on a good story with a problem that needs to be solved. Write a list of ideas. Choose a subject. Gather ideas for characters, plot, theme, and staging. Organize your ideas.

2

Creating Strong Characters

Choose one main character. Give that character one strong trait. Are they proud, smart, forgetful, or sloppy? Does this trait get the character into trouble?

3

Problems?

Take your main character and give them a problem. Write a sentence that tells about the character and their problem.

- A girl plays late with friends and misses her piano lesson.
- A boy doubts his sister is telling the truth.
- A girl feels that another girl doesn't like her.
- A boy needs to learn that he is old enough to take on a summer job.

4

Map It Out

Make a **story map** for the drama you would like to write. Be sure to include the main events. Who will be introduced? What will happen at the beginning of the story? What kind of problem will the main character face in the middle? What events solve the problem? How does the drama end?

First Draft

Use your notes from prewriting. Get your ideas down on paper. Do not worry about mistakes. This is just the first draft. Let your creative energy flow!

Ashley chose to write a drama about a brother and sister who think they've lost their dog. The brother blames the sister. The sister is mad at the brother for not believing her. Here is Ashley's first draft. It is not perfect, yet!

Act 1 (backyard of Sam and Melanie's house)
Melanie: Charlie. Come here Charlie.
Sam: (whistle)
Melanie: Charlie.
Sam (walking forward): The gate.
Melanie: Huh.
Sam: You left the gate open.
Melanie: Did not
Sam (pointing): Look.
Melanie: Charlie is gone. What if he gets lost and can't find his way home. What if someone picks him up and takes him back to their place?
Sam: We have to find him.
(Both run off stage)

Act 2
(Walking toward a bench in a park)
Sam: Charlie! Come on boy!
Melanie: We've looked everywhere, he's gone.
Sam: You should not have left the gate open.
Melanie: I did not. I promise, I did not.
Sam: You did. You are careless. Now we have lost our dog. It is all your fault.
Melanie: But I did not leave the gate open.
Sam (raising voice): You are a baby. You can not even close a simple gate.
Melanie (yelling): I am not a baby.
Dad (hear calling from a short distance away): Sam. Melanie.
Sam: Dad?
Dad (walking toward them): Mom was wondering where you went. She saw the back gate open and thought something had happened to make you go away.
Sam: She left the back gate open and Charlie is gone.
Dad: No she didn't. The lock is broken. I've been meaning to fix it. The wind blew it

open. Mom took Charlie to the dog groomers. Come on you two, we've got to get back home.
(All exit)

Act 3
(In backyard, standing beside closed gate)
Sam: I'm sorry I blamed you.
Melanie: Don't do it again.
Sam: I won't.
(Both walk offstage)

After your drama is finished, ask for feedback. Read your drama to a group of friends. Do they understand what is happening? Ask them if the drama makes sense? Does it have a strong beginning? What do they think of the ending?

6 Improving Your Work

Read your draft a couple of times.
Does it make sense? Decide what changes need to be made. List your characters. Add a few more stage directions. Polish the ending.

Characters: SAM (age 11), MELANIE (age 9 ½), DAD

Act 1 [*backyard of* SAM *and* MELANIE's *house*]

MELANIE (*holding dog leash*): Charlie! Come here Charlie!
SAM : (*whistles*)
MELANIE : Charleeeey. Don't you want to go for a walk, boy?
SAM (*walking forward*): The gate.
Melanie: Huh?
SAM : You left the gate open.
MELANIE : Did not!
SAM (*pointing*): Look.
MELANIE (*talking super fast*): Charlie's gone! What if he gets lost and can't find his way home? What if someone picks him up and takes him back to their place? What if he decides to go live with the wolves? What if…?
SAM (*cuts* MELANIE *off*): We have to find him. Let's go.
[*Both run off stage*]

Act 2 [*Walking toward a bench in a park*]

SAM : Charlie! Come on, boy!
MELANIE (*sits on bench, crying*): We've looked everywhere, he's gone.
SAM : You shouldn't have left the gate open.
MELANIE : I didn't. I promise, I didn't.
SAM : You did. You're careless. Now we've lost him. It's all your fault.
MELANIE : But I didn't leave it open.
SAM (*raising voice*): You're such a baby. Can't even close a simple gate.
MELANIE (*yelling*): I am not!
DAD (*hear calling from a short distance away*): Sam! Melanie!
SAM : Dad?
Dad (*walking toward them*): Mom was wondering where you went. She saw the back gate open.
MELANIE (*sobbing*): I didn't do it!
DAD : Do what?
SAM : She left the back gate open.
DAD : No, she didn't. The lock is broken. I've been meaning to fix it. The wind blew it open.
MELANIE : I told you!
SAM : But, Charlie's still gone!
DAD : Is that why you two are yelling at each other? Mom took Charlie to the dog groomers early this morning. He's still there. Come on you two, we've got to get back home. I've got a gate to fix.
[*All exit*]

Act 3 [*In backyard, standing beside closed gate*]

SAM : I'm sorry I blamed you.
MELANIE : I told you I didn't leave the gate open but you didn't listen.
SAM : I know. I was wrong this time. I promise to listen next time.
MELANIE (*following* SAM *as he walks off stage and talking super fast*): Next time? There won't be a next time. Brothers! You never listen. When I say I didn't do it, I didn't do it!

7

Checking All the Boxes

When you edit and proofread, make sure your writing is clear and accurate.

- Check your spelling.
- Fix punctuation mistakes.
- Fix capitalization mistakes.
- Fix grammar mistakes.

8

Spotlight, Please!

Write up a clean copy of your drama. Give it a title. Get a couple of friends together to help you act out the drama. Rehearse. Present the drama to your family.

Take a bow, Shakespeare! You have just written a drama!

Glossary

Please note: Some bold-faced words are defined in the text

character	The person or things that are speaking in the story
climax	The height of action or tension before the end of a story
conflict	A problem that the main character has to solve; a problem that causes trouble
dialogue	The words a character speaks
drama	A piece of writing that tells a story and is meant to be acted out
monologue	A piece of dialogue where only one character talks to an audience
moral	A life lesson taught through the drama
plot	The events that happen in the story
poetry	Short groups of words that tell a story
prose	A story written in sentences and paragraphs
resolution	The end of the story, when the plot's main problem is solved
script	The written work actors use to perform a drama
setting	The place and time that the story takes place
stage directions	The writing that tells characters when and where to move and how to say their lines
story map	A diagram that shows the basic parts of the plot
theme	The message of the story

Index

Further Resources

Books:

Much Ado About Nothing for Kids (Shakespeare Can Be Fun) by Lois Burdett. Firefly Books (2002)

Theatre for Young Audiences: 20 Great Plays for Children edited by Coleman A. Jennings. St. Martins Griffin (2005)

The BFG: A Set of Plays by Roald Dahl. Puffin (2007)

Websites:

Shakespeare for Kids: Folger Shakespeare Library
www.folger.edu/Content/Teach-and-Learn/Shakespeare-for-Kids/

Social Studies for Kids: Greek Tragedy – The Invention of Drama
www.socialstudiesforkids.com/articles/worldhistory/greektragedy.htm